SOUL'D OUT

Dying to Live

By
SHANE PRUITT

Foreword by Cliff Preston
Lead Singer of the band
Two Empty Chairs

Unless otherwise indicated, all Scripture quotations are taken
from the *Holy Bible*, New Living Translation, copyright 1996.
Used by permission of Tyndale House Publishers, Inc.,
P. O. Box 80, Wheaton, Illinois 60189.

British Library Cataloguing In Publication Data
A Record of this Publication is available
from the British Library

ISBN 978-1-84685-558-0

First Published 2007 by
Exposure Publishing, an imprint of Diggory Press

Diggory Press Ltd, Three Rivers, Minions,
Liskeard, Cornwall, PL14 5LE, UK
Affiliated to:
Diggory Press, Inc., of Goodyear, Arizona, USA
WWW.DIGGORYPRESS.COM

Contact Information:

Shane Pruitt
1604 Lost Crossing Trail
Arlington, TX   76002
burn4himministries@yahoo.com

website:
www.myspace.com/shanepruittministries

A special thank you to the Soul'd Out teenagers on
the front cover: Jenny Moscoso, Sarah Camp,
Chris McCain, Jennica Wanker, & Jimmy Dodd

Two Empty Chairs

Pick up a copy of their national debut album *Brighter Day*, available in early Spring of '07.

The band members: Wes Hymer (Bass and BGVs), Seth Bradham (Drums and BGVs), Josh Bryant (Guitars), and Cliff Preston (Lead Singer and Guitars) are very godly young men, who have tasted the blessings of God, and now they want to share what they have found with others.

Visit us on the web at:
www.twoemptychairs.com and
www.myspace.com/twoemptychairs

Call, write, or email these young men for more info:
Tonecrash Records
Attn: Marketing Department
5016 Spedale Ct, #329
Spring Hill, TN 37174
(615) 512-2143
info@tonecrashrecords.com

To my baby girl, Raygen, who I am praying will live a life that's Soul'd Out to Jesus!

Acknowledgements

This book is dedicated to my most valuable Treasure, Jesus Christ, and to those whose lives are Soul'd Out to Him.

To my soul mate, Kasi, thank you for praying for me and helping me keep what's most important, most important.

To my parents, family, friends, church family (Fellowship of Joy Student Ministry), Pastor Scott Camp, Pastor Guy Shafer, and everyone else who impacts the Kingdom of God!

To Dawn Yoder, thank you for reading and giving me insight during the early stages of this manuscript. You and your family are a blessing from the Father.

To Daniel Hancock and the Student Ministry at First Baptist Church of Grandview, TX. This book was born out of the Soul'd Out Disciple Now that I had the privilege of sharing. We saw God move in an amazing way!

FOREWORD

You can learn a lot from watching someone grow over the years. You learn the person's interests, wants, and needs. I have spent twenty-four years watching myself grow up. After all, God and I are the only people who can truly see what is happening in my life. I think back to a time in my life where a certain thing was king. The opportunity to play a game for a living was the most important thing to me. I was a Christian, sure, but my focus was being the best at what I did. It was soon stripped from my life and I thought I had lost it all. I had Soul'd Out to my childhood dream. It is okay to have dreams. God wants to give you your dreams. It is not okay to put those dreams before the One who gives them to you.

I met Shane Pruitt as God was showing me His plan for my life. I saw a guy who really had gone through similar situations as I had. We have had the chance of working together on a couple of occasions and I know that he is genuine. In a day and age where people are shying away from stepping on proverbial toes, Shane is saying what needs to be said. He is an inspiration in my life and I pray that you will let what God is saying through Shane sink in.

I challenge you to read the book through. Challenge yourself as you read it. I did, and it has already made a difference in my life. It is a guide of how to die to yourself, and how to live a full life. The only full life can be lived with God at the center.

This book will challenge believers and non-believers alike. I know from reading it myself, it made me look at some areas in my life that are so hard to let go. I understand that I have to give up all of it. I have to take up my cross daily. I have to die to myself. It is not about playing a game, or seeing how much we can get away with keeping. It is about realizing that God owns all of it anyway. What you think you can't live without can be taken in a moment. There is nothing on this earth worthy of you being Soul'd Out to. Jesus Christ paid the debt for us. He deserves our everything! God will be there in the end....will you?

Let's all put a "SOLD" sign in the front yard of our lives. To let the enemy know that we can't be bought, and to let others know we have stopped searching. We have found the one thing worth selling out to: Jesus Christ the Son of God.

Until They All Know,

Cliff Preston

Lead Singer of
Two Empty Chairs

CONTENTS

INTRODUCTION   13

Chapter 1
WE'RE ALL SOUL'D OUT TO SOMETHING   17

Chapter 2
SOMEONE WORTH FOLLOWING   29

Chapter 3
TIME TO DIE   43

Chapter 4
NOT FOR SALE   63

Chapter 5
I'M A FOLLOWER   79

BIBLIOGRAPHY   101

INTRODUCTION

"Yes, everything else is worthless when compared with the priceless gain of knowing Christ Jesus my Lord."
- Philippians 3:8a

THE English butcher and lay preacher Henry Varley, once told D. L. Moody, "The world has yet to see what God will do with a man fully consecrated to Him."[1] That statement bounced around in D. L.'s head, and it eventually became the driving force for him. From that day forward, he would strive to be that very man who would fully consecrate himself to the Father.

We know that eventually God used the unintelligent and uneducated Moody to lead over a million people to eternal salvation.

God Does Miracles Through Those Who Will Allow Him

---

[1] Bonnie C. Harvey, *D. L. Moody: The American Evangelist* (Uhrichsville, OH: Barbour Publishing Inc.), 7.

Dwight Lyman Moody's response to this challenge could be a powerful testimony to us all. When D. L. decided to be someone that was Soul'd Out, God began to do more through his life than he could have ever imagined. But isn't that what Scripture promises Christ will do with people who give all to Him? "Now to Him who is able to do exceedingly abundantly above all that we ask or think, according to the power that works in us." (Ephesians 3:20) How amazing are the miracles that God performs through the people who are absolutely Soul'd Out to Him!

The key truth to this scenario is that D. L. Moody never reached perfection in his life, and neither will we. As humans, we are not a perfect people, but we do have a perfect Savior in Christ Jesus. Mr. Moody understood this truth, so He completely depended on His Savior. Paul said it best in his letter to the Philippians, "I don't mean to say that I have already achieved these things or that I have already reached perfection! But I keep working toward that day when I will finally be all that Christ Jesus saved me for and wants me to be." (Philippians 3:12).

Where Are These Miracle Workers?

The cold, hard truth is that there is an almost invisible line between the Christian and the rest of the human race. Who are the saved, and who are the lost? Who are the sheep, and who are the goats? Who are the wheat, and who are the tares? Who are the dead men walking, and who are the walking dead? Frankly, it's impossible to tell who is who in America!

The Christian must be distinctly different from the non-Christian. A true follower of Christ declares Jesus as the most important Person in his or her life. Not only do true followers declare Jesus as most important, but they also live their lives with a desire to become more and more like Him every day. In short, it means to be completely Soul'd Out to Him!

We Are Called To Be Soul'd Out

In the Gospels, when Christ called people to follow Him, He only called them to be Soul'd Out followers. Nowhere did He call people to follow Him halfway. "Then Jesus said to His disciples, 'If anyone desires to come after Me, let him deny himself, and take up his cross, and follow Me.'" (Matthew 16:24)

Christ is calling you to be this kind of follower as well… one who is totally Soul'd Out!

It is my cry that we get back to the Gospel that changes the world by calling people to be absolutely Soul'd Out to the Son of God! A burden has been placed upon my heart to ask the question that stems directly from the statement Mr. Varley made to D. L. Moody, "What would happen if you became fully consecrated to God?" What would happen if this very statement would drive you to be Soul'd Out for Christ, as it drove D. L. Moody?

Will You Be Changed?

Through the reading of this small book, I hope that you will walk with me through Matthew 16:24, as we break down how important it is for us to be Soul'd Out to the Savior. I pray that your eyes will be opened through this study, and the work of the Father will become indescribable and immeasurable in your life! Choose this day Whom you will be Soul'd Out to!

Father, help me realize that You desire to use me for Your glory. Help me understand that You can only do the miraculous through me, if I am willing to give You first place in my life. Open my eyes and heart to You. - Amen

CHAPTER 1

WE'RE ALL SOUL'D OUT TO SOMETHING

"And the LORD God formed a man's body from the dust of the ground and breathed into it the breath of life. And the man became a living person." – Genesis 2:7

RIGHT now at this very moment, you my friend, are Soul'd Out! That's right, you! In fact, we're all Soul'd Out because that is the way we were created to be. When God breathed the breath of life into man, He created life that was to be Soul'd Out to Him. Your heart, your mind, your soul, and your strength were all created to be Soul'd Out to God. "Christ is the One through Whom God created everything in heaven and earth. He made the things we can see and the things we can't see – kings, kingdoms, rulers, and authorities. *Everything has been created through Him and FOR HIM.*" (Colossians 1:16)

I want you to know that this truth gives purpose to your life. I bet you didn't even realize that your life was that important. You may be saying to yourself, "My life sure does not feel like it has purpose! All I do is go to school and get loaded down with homework that my dog always eats." Or, "All I do is drag myself out of bed every morning, walk into my boring dead-end job, and stare at the clock waiting for my miserable day to be over with!"

Well, let me be the one to tell you that when you look at your reflection in the mirror with that tear sliding down your cheek (sniff-sniff) asking yourself, "Does this pathetic little life of mine have meaning?", allow me to be the one to tell you "YES, yes it does!" Your life is very, very important! It has purpose and meaning!

God has created you to be very special and unique. "Then God said, 'Let Us make people in Our image, to be like Ourselves. So God created people in His own image; God patterned them after Himself; male and female He created them (Genesis 1:26a & 27).'" I want you to know right now that you can begin to smile, because unlike any other creature in the world, you were created in the *Imago Dei*, Image of God.

What does it mean to be created in the Image of God? Warren Wiersbe had this to say about the Image of God: "Unlike the angels and the animals, humans can have a very special relationship with God. He not only gave us personality – minds to think with, emotions to feel with, and wills for making decisions – but He also gave us an inner spiritual nature that enables us to know Him and worship Him."[2]

We're Mostly Soul'd Out To Things Other Than God

Often this is the case for billions of people, and possibly even you. Like I said earlier, we are all Soul'd Out to something or someone, but very few of us are Soul'd Out to Christ. Scripture even recognizes this point: "But the gate to life is small, and the road is narrow, and only a few ever find it." (Matthew 7:14)

You may be saying to yourself right now, "This guy doesn't know me! I am not Soul'd Out to anything!"

Let me humbly reply by asking you to do me a favor. Would you just take a minute and answer these five simple questions?

---

[2] Warren W. Wiersbe, *The Bible Exposition Commentary: Pentateuch* (Colorado Springs, CO: Victor, 2001), p. 18.

1. What do you spend most of your time doing?
(Now answer)
2. What do you spend most of your time talking about?
(Now answer)
3. What do you spend most of your time thinking, or daydreaming about?
(Now answer)
4. What do you spend most of your money on?
(Now answer)
5. What excites you the most?
(Now answer)

Now do you have your answer to those five simple questions? It may be possible that you have more than one answer. But whatever your answer or answers were that, my friend, is what you are Soul'd Out to!

Let me lovingly, yet firmly, tell you that if your answer or answers to those questions were anything but Christ you are living a life that is not fulfilling its purpose for existence. Your life will always lack something.

Rick Warren expressed it best in *The Purpose Driven Life* when he said, "Without a clear purpose, you will keep changing directions, jobs, relationships, churches, or other externals – hoping each change will settle the confusion or fill the emptiness in your heart."[3]

---

[3] Rick Warren, *The Purpose Driven Life* (Grand Rapids, MI: Zondervan Publishing, 2002), 32.

You may be saying, "The answers to my questions were things that were actually good, or things that are definitely not harmful, such as my family, sports, my job, my boyfriend or girlfriend, academics, hobbies, singing, etc."

Can I tell you something? You are exactly right. None of those things are sinful, or necessarily harmful in themselves. However, when you elevate any of them to the highest place in your heart, then you've gone way too far! And you, my friend, have placed yourself on very dangerous ground physically and spiritually.

You are in danger physically, because all of these things can be taken from you in a split-second. I can't help but recall the story of a young man that I went to high school with. He and his girlfriend dated from the eighth grade all the way through high school. She had become his world. You would never see her without him close by. This young man had fallen head-over-heels in love with this young girl, and he had become completely and fully Soul'd Out to her.

However, this story ends tragically like many do. After high school she went off to a university, and he stayed in Waco to work. She went from coming home every weekend to spend time with him to eventually calling him with the news that she had found someone else. This young man could not take a blow like this because she had dangerously become his whole world. In his eyes, he had lost it all, and life no longer had any meaning without her. So he took a 22-caliber handgun, placed it on his chest over his heart, and ended it. In the suicide letter to his mom, he wrote, "My heart is hurting so bad that I have to end the pain!"

Situations like this remind me of the verses Jesus spoke from the Sermon on the Mount. "Anyone who listens to my teaching and obeys Me is wise, like a person who builds a house on the solid rock. Though the rain comes in torrents and the floodwaters rise and the winds beat against that house, it won't collapse, because it is built on rock. But anyone who hears my teaching and ignores it is foolish, like a person who builds a house on sand. When the rains and floods come and the winds beat against that house, it will fall with a mighty crash." (Matthew 7:24 - 27)

Whatever you are Soul'd Out to is ultimately what you are building your house on. If you are Soul'd Out to anything other than Christ, then you are building your house on sand. It will eventually slide out from under your feet, and you will fall very hard. If you're building your house on people it's very possible for them to be taken from you. If you are building your house on sports, you should know that injuries happen all the time. If you're Soul'd Out to your job people get fired and laid off every day. And so on and so on...

Spiritually, this is also very dangerous, because you have placed that object on the throne of your heart as your god, breaking the first commandment of God, which says, "Do not worship any other gods besides me." (Exodus 20:3) By doing this, you have decided to exchange God for something far less valuable. "Instead of believing what they knew was the truth about God, they deliberately chose to believe lies. So they worshipped the things God made but not the Creator Himself, Who is to be praised forever." (Romans 1:25) You have exchanged God for something that He has created for your pleasure, not your worship!

Another dangerous fact about being Soul'd Out to anything other than God is: whatever you are Soul'd Out to, is eventually what you will become. It is what defines you. Louie Giglio said, "Whatever you worship, you imitate; whatever you imitate, you become."[4] Bluntly put: eventually you will become whatever you're Soul'd Out to. If you evaluate your life and you don't like what you see or what you are becoming, then

---

[4] Louie Giglio, *The Air I Breathe* (Sisters, OR: Multnomah Publishers, INC., 2003), 33.

maybe you should really consider what you are being Soul'd Out to!

You'll Never Be Fully Satisfied

As I said before, whatever it is that you have become Soul'd Out to, and have exchanged God for, will never fully satisfy you. Because of Adam and Eve's rebellion in the Garden of Eden, every boy and every girl, except for One, (believe me when I say you are not that One), was born with a nature that is inclined to sin. King David exclaimed in his Psalm of repentance, "For I was born a sinner – yes, from the moment my mother conceived me." (Psalm 51:5)

This sin nature has caused every single one of us to be born with this huge God-shaped hole in our soul, which only He can fill. Billions of people have lived their entire lives trying to fill this hole with things other than God. Many people try to fill it with success, money, possessions, athletics, family, boys, girls, etc. While others try to fill this hole with alcohol, drugs, pornography, sexual immorality, hurting themselves or hurting others, etc.

Allow me to be the one to plead with you to understand that nothing, absolutely nothing will satisfy you, because there is nothing that will fill that hole completely.

24

It terrifies me to think of it like this: Have you ever put together a 1000 piece puzzle only to find at the end, there is one huge piece missing right in the middle of the puzzle? That has to be one of the lowest feelings in the world, right? You have spent literally days, sometimes weeks putting together this elaborate puzzle, only to throw it away in the end because it is no good without the final piece.

This pathetic little illustration doesn't even come close to what it is like to live a whole life putting it together like an elaborate puzzle, and at the end be missing the main centerpiece, Jesus Christ. In fact, Scripture tells us that a life not lived with Christ at the center of it, is not a life at all! "The sin of this one man, Adam, caused death to rule over us, but all who receive God's wonderful, gracious gift of righteousness will live in triumph over sin and death through this one man, Jesus Christ." (Romans 5:17) If you're not Soul'd Out to the Savior, you're not truly living at all!

I want you to do something for yourself right now. I want you to recall your answer, or answers from the five questions above. I want you to figuratively place your answer, or answers, in your hand right now, and stare at it. Are you looking? Are you staring at your answer?

If that in your hand right now is anything other than Christ, I want you to look at your hand and say out loud to that object or objects, "I am Soul'd Out to you! And you are taking my life from me! I refuse to be Soul'd Out to you any longer!" You may have to repeat this several times to grasp the realness of this desperate situation. I want you to do what you have to do to make this reality sink in. "You are taking life from me! And you will never fully satisfy me!"

You Get One Shot

Whether you're young or old, male or female, rich or poor, you must realize that this is your one and only life. This is the only chance you have to get it right by being Soul'd Out to the right Person. It's eye-opening to read what Louie Giglio had to say in his book, *The Air I Breathe:* "You have one brief opportunity in time to declare your allegiance, to unleash your affection, to exalt something or Someone above all else."[5]

How will you spend the rest of your life? Who or what will you be Soul'd Out

---

[5] Louie Giglio, *The Air I Breathe*, 29.

to?   How you answer will ultimately determine how you spend eternity.

You should know that Jesus Christ is calling you to be Soul'd Out to Him. Let's take a journey to see how He can fill that hole in our soul, since you only have one shot at this life.

Verses to Meditate On:

"You watched me as I was being formed in utter seclusion, as I was woven together in the dark of the womb.   You saw me before I was born.   Every day of my life was recorded in Your book.   Every moment was laid out before a single day had passed."

- Psalm 139:15 - 16

"For we are God's masterpiece.   He has created us anew in Christ Jesus, so that we can do the good things He planned for us long ago."

- Ephesians 2:10

"You are worthy, O Lord our God Almighty – the One who always was, who is, and who is still to come."

- Revelation 4:11

"If you try to keep your life for yourself, you will lose it.   But if you give up your life for Me, you will find true life."

- Matthew 16:25

"Then Jesus said to the disciples, 'If any of you wants to be my follower, you must put aside your selfish ambition, shoulder your cross, and follow Me. If you try to keep your life for yourself, you will lose it. But if you give up your life for Me, you will find true life.'"

- Matthew 16:24 - 25

Father, I pray that You will lead me on this journey to see what it means to be Soul'd Out to You. I pray that You will change my life from being Soul'd Out to things other than You! Allow me to know You, and to live a life that honors You! - Amen

CHAPTER 2

SOMEONE WORTH FOLLOWING

*"Then Jesus said to the disciples, 'If any of you wants to be My follower...'" –
Matthew 16:24*

As Soul'd Out people, we will commit our lives to whatever we believe is most important to us. Believe it or not, you spend your entire life chasing after whatever you are Soul'd Out to. We all have that idol in our life that's saying, "If you want me, then come and chase after me! Be my follower." And we will respond dumbly by saying, "Yes, yes! You are most important to me, and I am going to do whatever you want me to! I will be your follower."

Whatever you determined in Chapter One to be most important to you, whether it be your family, boyfriend or girlfriend, sports, popularity, alcohol, lust, etc., you have declared that "thing" as your most valuable treasure of all. You're Soul'd Out to what you value the most!

To change what you're Soul'd Out to, you must find a treasure that is far more valuable than any treasure you already have. What you need to save your life is to come across a treasure that makes all your other treasures look small and insignificant. When faced with that Treasure, you will be more than willing to trade all others for that one.

Valuable Treasures

One day I was in my office at the church, and decided to type in the key-word search box on the Internet: "the world's most expensive." I was curious to see what would pop up. What I found was very interesting.

A company in Switzerland owns the most expensive watch in the world. The watch contains three heart-shaped diamonds: a pink heart diamond which weighs 15 carats, a blue heart diamond which weighs 12 carats, and a white heart diamond which weighs 11 carats. These three diamonds are set in a bracelet with more white and yellow diamonds that make up little flowers in design. In total the watch carries over 200 carats of diamonds, and an estimated value of 25 million

dollars.[6] This is a very valuable
treasure!

I also came across the most expensive pair of shoes in the world. The Cinderella Slippers are designed by Stuart Weitzman. They are one-of-a-kind 4 ½ inch stiletto sandals studded with 565 platinum-set Kwiat diamonds. The sandals also include 55 carats of clear diamonds, and one big 5 carat stone. These shoes are worth an estimated value of 2 million dollars.[7] What valuable treasures these shoes are!

Lastly, I came across the world's most expensive hotel room. A single night in the Bridge Suite at the Atlantis resort in the Bahamas, will cost you $25,000. In fact, this rate is based on a typical 21-hour stay (2 P.M. check-in and 11 A.M. checkout), and this rate breaks down to a womping $1,190 an hour.[8] What an expensive treasure this hotel room is!

Although these treasures are very valuable and impressive, they're still not the most valuable. These treasures can't

---

[6] *"The Most Expensive Watch in the World"*, Tyler – Adams Corporation: Official Website, available from http://www.tyler-adam.com; Internet; accessed 9 May 2005.

[7] *"The World's Most Expensive Shoes"*, rediff.com: Official Website, available from http://www.rediff.com; Internet; accessed 9 May 2005.

[8] *"The World's Most Expensive Hotel Rooms"*, Forbes.com: Official Website, available from http://www.forbes.com; Internet; accessed 9 May 2005.

change your life, nor can they keep you from death. If you lived your life Soul'd Out to one of these million-dollar gems, you would still die, and it would remain for someone else to be Soul'd Out to.

Isn't it heartbreaking to realize that these treasures are some of the best that this world has to offer, and yet they can't do anything significant for you? "And how do you benefit if you gain the whole world but lose your own soul in the process? Is anything worth more than your soul?" (Matthew 16:26)

Jesus: The Greatest Treasure of All

"The Kingdom of Heaven is like a treasure that a man discovered hidden in a field. In his excitement, he hid it again and sold everything he owned to get enough money to buy the field - and to get the treasure, too!

Again, the Kingdom of Heaven is like a pearl merchant on the lookout for choice pearls. When he discovered a pearl of great value, he sold everything he owned and bought it!"

- Matthew 13:44-46

In these two parables, Jesus is comparing the Kingdom of Heaven to a hidden treasure and a pearl of great value. Something you must realize about parables is that every parable has one main point that it is trying to convey. Both of these parables are teaching the same important lesson that there is a Treasure out there that's worth trading everything for!

Notice in the first parable there is a man who is minding his own business. This man could have either been working in the field, or possibly he was just walking through. Whatever the situation was, he stumbled upon a very, very valuable treasure.

I can just picture this guy in my mind tripping over this treasure that was sticking out of the ground, and yelling out in pain because he had stumped his toe. He turns around to see what he tripped over, kneels down to get a closer look, then digs out the dirt around it. He pulls the treasure up with glaring eyes and a smiling face, and yells out, "Wow! I must have this treasure! Now that I have encountered this treasure, my life will be worthless unless I possess it. Possessing this treasure will absolutely change my life!"

So he buries it again, runs home and sells everything he has. The man cashes in his life savings, all his possessions, and then buys the whole field; just so that he could have this very valuable treasure.

The second parable is just a little different. Instead of stumbling over a treasure, this man was seeking one. However, the result of his find was the same as the first guy, because he traded all he knew for this one treasure. This particular man was a jewelry dealer who traded in pearls. He looked for valuable pearls, bought them, and then sold them for a profit. But, one day he came across a pearl that far surpassed any pearl he had ever seen before, so he considered it a fair exchange to trade everything he had to own it.

Did you catch the teaching point in both of these parables? If you didn't get the main point, let me help you: the old was exchanged for the new. The men found something that was worth following and being Soul'd Out to. They compared the treasure to their individual lives, and decided that their lives paled in comparison to possessing this new find.

Each of the men had to have their treasure once they were exposed to it! They were more than willing to trade their old lives, so that they could be Soul'd Out to their new treasure.

So what is this treasure that's so valuable? Well, both of these parables say that the Kingdom of Heaven is. The Kingdom of Heaven is a term that is descriptive of any type of ruler ship that God may assert here on earth. However, we know that the absolute rule of God on earth will not occur until the Second

Coming of Christ. So that means the Kingdom of Heaven in these two parables must be talking about the absolute rule of God in an individual's life.

However, it's a very disturbing truth that God doesn't have absolute rule in our lives because our lives are tainted by sin.

We've all done things that we know are wrong and are not pleasing to a holy God. Whether we've been Soul'd Out to things other than Christ, told lies, stolen things, disobeyed our parents, etc., the truth is we're all dirty-dog-sinners! "For all have sinned; all fall short of God's glorious standard." (Romans 3:23) We are naturally rebellious against God.

God can't rule in our lives because of our sin. The Good News is that the Son of God, Jesus Christ, came to be sin for us. He was the perfect Sacrifice when He laid down His life on the cross. While Jesus hung on a cruel Roman cross, God the Father was punishing His Son, as if He had committed every sin of every person who ever lived. "He was wounded and crushed for our sins. He was beaten that we might have peace. He was whipped, and we were healed! All of us have strayed away like sheep. We have left God's paths to follow our own. Yet the Lord laid on Him the guilt and sins of us all." (Isaiah 53:5 – 6)

However, three days later, Jesus arose from the dead. When He came back to life, it signified that God the Father accepted God the Son's sacrifice on your behalf and my behalf. Jesus Christ conquered our sin, death, and the rule of Satan in our lives. He made the way possible to be Soul'd Out to God. If we would trade our lives like the two men did in the parables by claiming Christ as our most valuable Treasure, and put our complete trust in Him, we could have all these benefits! "For the wages of sin is death, but the free gift of God is eternal life through Christ Jesus our Lord." (Romans 6:23)

Jesus Christ, the Son of God, is the most valuable Treasure of all because He is the only One who can bring the Kingdom of Heaven. He is the only One who can take our sins away through our repentance and faith in Him, and He is the only One who can make all things new. "He has removed our rebellious acts as far away from us as the east is from the west." (Psalm 103:12) "What this means is that those who become Christians become new persons. They are not the same anymore, for the old life is gone. A new life has begun." (2 Corinthians 5:17)

You see, it doesn't really matter how precious or valuable an earthly treasure is. A pearl, a diamond, a watch, shoes, a hotel room, etc. None of them can offer anything truly worthwhile or lasting. They cannot heal a broken relationship, give peace to a troubled mind, or forgive a sinful heart. They offer little to the present, and nothing for the future. Absolutely nothing compares to Jesus. He is the only One who can offer forgiveness, love, peace, joy, purity, righteousness, and eternal life. He is worth following and being Soul'd Out to!

My Story

Football and football cards were my life from around the age of eight to fourteen. I loved both tremendously, but the Miami Dolphins would cause a great manifestation of this love. Now when I was growing up, if you loved the Miami Dolphins then it was most likely a guarantee that you loved Dan "The Man" Marino! All of these components caused a deep hunger within me to get a hold of every Dan Marino football card I could possibly get my hands on. I remember building up a glorious collection of Marino football cards that I was very proud of!

However, I was slapped in the face one day with a horrible reality. My Dan Marino card collection that was once so awesome and complete was now puny and empty. "Why?" you ask. Because I came across the Dan Marino rookie card, and I did not have it!

If you don't know what a rookie card is, it is the very first football card that comes out as soon as a player turns pro. The rookie card is usually the rarest and most valuable card of that certain player.

I remember looking at my collection and my heart sank. Without that Dan Marino rookie card, I had nothing! It was odd to me that the same card collection that I was once so proud of, and boasted to all of my friends about, was now very tainted to me. I had become very discouraged because the collection that I had now would never amount to much if it did not include that rookie card. I needed that card to be the cornerstone of my collection!

As I got older, my passions and interests changed a bit. Oh, I still loved Dan Marino and the Miami Dolphins, but now sports, girls, parties, and religion took the place of football cards.

In high school I built a life that all young men in small country towns were supposed to have. I played sports, and wore my letter jacket covered in patches proudly. I would use girls for my own pleasure because that is how you became the hero of the locker room. I remember pathetically boasting about how I could party with the best of them because I could put a ton of beer away before ever passing out or getting sick. Sadly enough that's how a man is measured, right? By how many beers he can drink and still walk without vomiting?

Oh, and I had religion too. I could pass off a hangover just well enough to come to church, and be a leader in my church youth group. Sometimes I would cut off my partying a half-hour short, so I could come home and prepare some "makeshift Bible study" to teach to a Sunday school class of my peers. I was living a lie. I would tell the people in my class not to do the things that I had just done the night before.

This was a life that I had become very proud of. I had everything I needed, and I had it in order!

Then one day I was slapped in the face with a horrible reality. My life, which was once in order and so complete, was now in such a mess and so empty. "Why?" you ask. Because I came across Jesus Christ, the Son of God, and I did not have Him! I looked at my life, and my heart sank because without this Jesus I had nothing. The cold hard truth was that I knew a lot about God, but I did not know Him.

You know what? I ended up getting that Dan Marino rookie card and I still have it today, but it cost me a lot of cards to get it and I believe that it was worth it.

I also want you to know something else about me that is a lot more important than a rookie card. I also now have Jesus Christ as my Lord and Savior, and it cost me much more than football cards. It cost me my old life. But you know what? It's worth it, because I now realize that He is the most valuable Treasure of all! He's worth being Soul'd Out to!

Is He The Most Valuable Treasure To You?

Have you ever laid it all down to possess Him? Can you say that you're truly Soul'd Out to Him? Is He honestly the most valuable Treasure to you, or does something else take His place? Take some time right now to meditate on these questions.

Understand today that the Son of God is offered to everyone. No matter how poor or how rich you are. It doesn't matter if you're white, black, Asian, Spanish, etc. It doesn't matter if your hair is long, shaggy, short, or if you have no hair at all.

Christ is offered to those who have nice clothes, or those with ragged clothes. It doesn't matter if you're a country boy, city boy, business girl, or skater girl. The Son of God is calling every single one of us to be His followers, and He is well worth it! However, there is a price, and it's the same for everyone: simply all they have!

Verses to Meditate On:

"We cannot imagine the power of the Almighty, yet He is so just and merciful that He does not oppress us. No wonder people everywhere fear Him. People who are truly wise show Him reverence."

- Job 37:23-24

"O Lord, our Lord, the majesty of Your name fills the earth! Your glory is higher than the heavens."

- Psalm 8:1

"How precious is Your unfailing love, O God! All humanity finds shelter in the shadow of Your wings."

- Psalm 36:7

"Because of this, God raised Him up to the heights of heaven and gave Him a name that is above every other name, so that at the name of Jesus every knee will bow, in heaven and on earth and under the earth, and every tongue will confess that Jesus Christ is Lord, to the glory of God the Father."

- Philippians 2:9-11

"And a voice from heaven said, 'This is My beloved Son, and I am fully pleased with Him.'"

                                      - Matthew 3:17

Father, thank You for opening my eyes to how valuable You really are. Because of Jesus Christ, my sins can be removed from me as far as the east is from the west. I have recognized that He is worth following because only through Him can I become a new person. Only because of His obedience on the cross, taking my place, can I be Soul'd Out to You.

Lord, please continue to open my eyes, heart, mind, and soul to the necessity of having You as number one in my life. – Amen.

CHAPTER 3

TIME TO DIE

"you must put aside your selfish ambition..." - Matthew 16:24

DID you realize that today the average life span is 25,550 days? That is approximately how many days you will receive if you are blessed enough to live a full life. You should also know that God has created you to live every single one of those days to the fullest. He desires for you to live life looking at each new day as an opportunity and adventure where you can impact eternity by serving Him.

However, you have two very strong enemies out there trying to stop you from living your life in this way. These two enemies want you to focus your life on any goal that excludes being Soul'd Out to Christ.

Your greatest enemy is not that bully from your eighth grade year, but rather it's Satan, and he is out to completely devour you. "Be careful! Watch out for attacks from the Devil, your great enemy.

He prowls around like a roaring lion, looking for some victim to devour." (1 Peter 5:8)

His main goal is to make sure you don't live a life that's Soul'd Out to God. This enemy wants to crush you, destroy you, and to keep you just busy enough to be too busy for Christ. By doing this, Satan knows that you will end up wasting your life on things that are fading away, and will eventually spend an eternity with him separated from God. "Then the Devil, who betrayed them, was thrown into the lake of fire that burns with sulfur, joining the beast and the false prophet. There they will be tormented day and night forever and ever. And anyone whose name was not found recorded in the Book of Life was thrown into the lake of fire (Revelation 20:10, 15)." Unfortunately, if you have never denied yourself and given your life to Christ, then this will be your fate as well.

Our second greatest enemy that keeps us from being Soul'd Out to God is ourselves, because through acts of selfishness we often don't live a life that honors Christ above all else. That's right! I'm going to be bold enough to say it, because you're not here to hit me. "Your greatest enemy, besides Satan, is yourself. You get in the way of God's work in your life! If you could take yourself out of the picture, God would do the miraculous in your life."

You Must Die

You get in the way of what God wants to do in your life. He wants to use you for His glory, but your selfish ambitions won't allow Him to be number one in your life. None of us will admit it openly, but our well-being is our top priority. We are all completely in love with ourselves.

I know by now you're probably upset with me, saying out loud, "That's not true! I always put myself last! I put the needs of my family, my friends, my job, and my church all before my needs!" Well, let me respond with two statements: "Stop arguing with a book because people around you are looking at you like you're crazy! And, I'm sorry, but you do put yourself first."

Think about this:

- When you get hungry, what do you do? You feed yourself.
- When you get thirsty, you get yourself something to drink.
- When you're cold, you find a way to warm yourself.
- When someone says something very hurtful to you or about you; you get very offended and upset. Why? Because

they did something to you that threatens your pride and self-image.
- When someone tries to harm you physically, you fight back. Why? Because your well being is in danger.
- And etc., etc., etc. I could give examples for hours.

Please don't think that I am pointing a finger at you like some overly pious priest or self-righteous minister. Most likely I'm more guilty about this than you are. I just wanted you to see that, contrary to popular opinion, Americans don't have a self-esteem problem. In fact, we have a problem of loving ourselves way too much!

We live our lives asking self-centered questions like, "What do I want to be?" Or, "What should I do with my life?" Or, "What are my goals, my ambitions, my dreams for my future?"[9] However, you must realize that this life is not about you! The purpose for your existence goes way beyond your own personal fulfillment, your happiness, or your success. Your life is meant to impact all of eternity. "For we are God's masterpiece. He has created us anew in Christ Jesus, so that we can do the good

---

[9] Rick Warren, *The Purpose Driven Life* (Grand Rapids, MI: Zondervan Publishing Company, 2002), 17.

things He planned for us long ago." (Ephesians 2:10)

If your life is going to fulfill the purpose of its existence, you must die. You must be able to testify about your life the way Paul testified about his, when he said, "I myself no longer live, but Christ lives in me. So I live my life in this earthly body by trusting in the Son of God, who loved me and gave Himself for me." (Galatians 2:20)

To be Soul'd Out to God, you must come to the point in your life where you're willing to die to yourself. You must be willing to put aside your selfish ambitions, and make God's will your top priority. It is no longer about your hopes, dreams, and aspirations, but rather it is about God's glory. You declare that God is in control of every step you take. He's in control of who you marry, what you do, and how you use your time and talents. He is to be in control of every single area of your life because it is no longer you who lives, but rather He who lives through you.

A Foot In Both Worlds

Sadly, there are many people who try to live with a foot in both worlds. When you honestly evaluate the people who fill our church's pews, you will find that many marvel at the wonderful things of Jesus Christ, but they don't take anything to heart. There are many church members who want to follow the Son of God at a distance and be thrilled and entertained, but there are very few who are ever changed and become completely Soul'd Out to Him.

I have seen this tragedy played out over and over again during my ministry. Folks would get so excited about conferences, camps, Disciple-Now's, revivals, and concerts. However, when it came time to completely give Christ control of their habits, friends, and those pesky "secret areas" of their lives, they decided to walk away instead. There were many who were quick to jump on the bandwagon of Christianity, but as soon as the cause became unpopular or demanding, they would jump off! Tragically, it reminds me of the verse in 1 John that says, "These people left our churches because they never really belonged with us; otherwise, they would have stayed with us. When they left us, it proved that they do not belong with us." (1 John 2:19) These people were never true followers, nor were they ever truly Soul'd Out.

A true follower, one who is going to be Soul'd Out, must be fully committed to Christ, not trying to live with one foot in both worlds.

I remember one day as a young boy going exploring with one of my buddies down at a river that was close to my parents' house. We were crossing a pasture full of cattle, and as we got to the river, we came up to an electric fence that was designed to keep animals away by shocking them if they got too close. I will never forget my friend saying, "Hey, man, you go through the fence first. I will hold one part of the fence down with my shoe, and the other part up with a stick."

And here I go very dumbly through the fence with our plan in hand. I came to a vulnerable point, where I had one foot in a very safe world (a pasture that was my dad's and that was safe), and I had the other foot in a very dangerous world (an area that was actually posted with a No Trespassing sign, and was quite dangerous). I was literally trying to stand with a foot in both worlds while I was straddling this fence.

Then it happened, as you can imagine. My friend, who was holding one part of the fence down with his foot while holding the other part up with a stick, somehow got shocked by the fence. Once he was shocked he let go and forgot all about me. I had a foot in both worlds and I'm sure you can tell the rest of this story. It was a very shocking experience!

This ridiculous illustration that depicted a serious tragedy is nothing in comparison to what happens to those who try to live with a foot in both worlds spiritually. You can't have the attitude that says you are going to follow Christ, yet do your own thing as well (which is ultimately saying that you are going to serve yourself). "No one can serve two masters. For you will hate one and love the other, or be devoted to one and despise the other." (Matthew 6:24)

You must realize that you can't follow Christ "just a little bit." You are either fully committed to Christ, or you are not committed at all. You are either completely Soul'd Out to Him, or you're completely Soul'd Out to something else. "Anyone who isn't helping Me opposes Me, and anyone who isn't working with Me is actually working against Me." (Matthew 12:30)

Beginning to Understand?

If you are still reading this book, I honestly believe that you're very interested in what we've been talking about, and by now you are beginning to comprehend that you can't be Soul'd Out to the Savior of the world without first putting aside your selfish ambitions. I know by now that I've pushed the truth that you can't follow Christ and also have the attitude that you're going to do things your way.

If you truly realize these truths from above, then I must ask you some serious questions. Why are you not absolutely head-over-heels in love and infatuated with Jesus Christ to the point where He is number one in your life, without any competition from anything else? Why are you not completely Soul'd Out to the Son of God? What's your excuse?

People Of Excuses

In the gospel of Luke, there are three men from whom we can learn valuable lessons. They were men of excuses who decided that being Soul'd Out to Christ would interfere too much with their personal agendas, so they chose not to follow Him. Each man had an excuse as to why he could not be Soul'd Out to the Son of God, and I can only imagine the depth of their regrets as they suffer eternal punishment as you read this.

Let's take a look and learn from their mistakes:

Contestant #1

"As they were walking along someone said to Jesus, 'I will follow you no matter where you go.' But Jesus replied, 'Foxes have dens to live in, and birds have nests, but I, the Son of Man, have no home of my own, not even a place to lay my head."

- Luke 9:57-58

Here we have Contestant #1. He runs up to Jesus exclaiming that he's ready to follow Christ wherever He may go. However, the Son of God looked straight into the heart of this man, and saw that he was not really serious. This should be an eye-opening reality to every single one of us who makes superficial commitments to God, because He knows what is really going on in our hearts!

Jesus responded to this man that foxes have comfort and security in the shelter of their dens. Also, birds have the same comforts and securities by being able to return to their nests every evening. However, Jesus explained that He had a mission of spreading the Gospel of the Kingdom of God.

The Son of Man was constantly on the move and did not have the comforts and securities of a steady home. There were many nights that Jesus slept on the ground, and in other people's homes.

It was as if Jesus looked at this man and said, "Are you willing to do this as well, and follow Me wherever I go? Are you willing to leave the comforts and securities of your home? Do you still want to follow Me even though it is extremely difficult and uncomfortable at times?"

We can only assume that this man said, "No, thanks. That is just too hard, and I like to be comfortable. I think I changed my mind, because I thought it would be a lot easier." Contestant #1, Excuse #1, and Failure #1. What is your excuse?

Contestant #2

"He said to another person, 'Come, be my disciple.' The man agreed, but he said, 'Lord, first let me return home and bury my father.' Jesus replied, 'Let those who are spiritually dead care for their own dead. Your duty is to go and preach the coming of the Kingdom of God.'"

- Luke 9:59-60

Here we have Contestant #2. This situation is a little different because Jesus approaches this man, instead of the other two situations where the men approached Him. He calls this young man to be His disciple, and to preach the coming of the Kingdom of God. However, the man responds, "Lord, first let me return home and bury my father (v. 59b)."

At first, this response by the man seems to be harmless and credible. After all, this is what a good boy should do, right? Go home and bury his dead father.

If this young man were doing the right thing, then why in the world would Jesus reply to him the way He did?

The Son of God responded this way because He knew that this man's father was not dead yet. It is highly unlikely that the father was already dead and the son was merely asking permission to finish the funeral. If that were the case, the son would have been nowhere near Jesus - hardly on the road where Jesus was walking - because he would have been home with the other mourners.[10]

His dad was most likely an elderly man who was entering into his last stages of life. This guy wanted to go home and hang out with his father until he died. The man's main concern was to get his father's inheritance. He was afraid that if he followed Jesus, then he would miss out on what was supposed to be coming to him.

Now you can see why Jesus responded to him the way He did. He knew that the father wasn't dead yet. The Son of God may have been implying, "There are others who can take care of your father for now. My call is more important!"

However, we can assume that this man felt that receiving his inheritance and material possessions were more important

---

[10] Bruce B. Harvey, Dave Veerman, & Linda K. Taylor, *Life Application Bible Commentary: Luke* (Wheaton, IL: Tyndale House Publishers Inc., 1997), 262.

at that stage in his life. I can picture him saying, "Jesus, I just can't do it right now. Let me do these things first, and then I will catch You later on. Doing these other things is more important than preaching the Kingdom of God. It is just not a good time yet."

Contestant #2, Excuse #2, and Failure #2. What is your excuse?

Contestant #3

"Another said, 'Yes, Lord, I will follow You, but first let me say good-bye to my family.' But Jesus told him, 'Anyone who puts a hand to the plow and then looks back is not fit for the Kingdom of God.'"

-     Luke 9:61-62

Lastly, we have Contestant #3. This situation is very similar to the first contestant because this man runs up to Jesus and proclaims his commitment. Although he declares his allegiance, it is all for naught, because he threw in a clause as if he were the one who was in control of Christ's calling.

This man told the Son of God, "I am going to follow You, but let me first go back and tell my family good-bye." In a sense, he was saying, "I'm going to follow you, Jesus, but first let me go back to my old life. Let me dabble in some things from my past for a little bit; then I'm all Yours!"

Christ's response is very frightening for those people who have made a profession of faith at a time in their life. They follow Him for a little while, and then go back to their old lifestyles. "Anyone who puts a hand to the plow and then looks back is not fit for the Kingdom of God." (v. 62)

Jesus used the example of a plowman working in a field, and compared it to working in the Kingdom of God. It is always the goal of the plowman to run a straight line when he is getting ready to plant seed for the harvest. If a man hooks up his plow to a donkey or an ox, and then constantly looks back as he works, it will prove to be disastrous in accomplishing his goal.

It reminds me of the time I was driving down a road near our church in my wife's new car. As I was driving about 35 miles per hour, I began to smell something vicious coming from the back seat. I turned completely around while still driving to notice my old basketball shoes from the men's game the previous night in the floorboard. After I figured out that it was my shoes that were putting off toxic fumes, I turned back around to notice that I had not been driving a straight line. I fixed my eyes back on the path just in time to hit the curb, and blow my tire out!

I was now stuck on the side of the road changing my tire. As I was changing my tire with the pathetic little tools that the factory puts in your car for times such as these, I could not help but think about Luke 9:62. I went from going in the right direction, to looking behind me, to straying off the path, to not moving at all.

That is what Jesus was teaching this young man. If a person allows anything to hold him back from full allegiance to Christ, then he or she is not fit for the Kingdom of God. You can't follow Christ and continue to dip back into your old lifestyle or your previous sins. You will eventually end up on the side of the road going nowhere!

We can only assume that this man did the same as the other two did. "Jesus, I just can't do that! Oh, I will do it, but just not right now. I have some things I need to do first. Let me go back to my lifestyle and the things I am familiar with one last time!"

What this man did not understand was that he is not the one who lays down the terms for discipleship, because the Son of God does that. Also, only those who are completely Soul'd Out are true disciples of Christ!

Contestant #3, Excuse #3, and Failure #3.

What is Your Excuse?

Maybe your story is very similar to one of these three contestants. Possibly you are saying, "I will be Soul'd Out to Christ, but just not right now. I have some things I want to do first. I am going to wait until I get older, because I want to be able to 'sow my wild oats first.' I want to party it up while I am still young. I have time to get serious about God later on."

Maybe these statements do not apply to you, but let me ask you: What is your excuse? Think about it for a minute… Is your excuse worth getting in the way of God's will for your life?

Allow me to give you two points to think about. First, Jesus is calling you to be absolutely Soul'd Out to Him right now, but your excuses have to be put to the side. You must realize that your life is not about you, and the moment you realize that, you will run out of excuses. You must die to yourself, and you must die to your excuses.

Make a statement today that your life is going to fulfill its purpose, and you are going to live for God's glory without allowing any excuse to get in your way!

Secondly, please do not rely on the excuse that you will wait a little while longer, and then you will be Soul'd Out to Christ. The sad truth is that there are millions of people who sincerely intend on being Soul'd Out "one day," but the reality is that none of us is promised that "one day." You are not promised tomorrow, and you don't have the guarantee that you can wait until later!

David wrote, "Lord, remind me how brief my time on earth will be. Remind me that my days are numbered, and that my life is fleeing away." (Psalm 39:4) God has numbered every single one of our days. He knows the very second that you will draw your last breath. Recognize right now that your days are numbered, and every day that goes by gets closer to the magical day when you will draw your last breath.

I will close this chapter by asking you to do me a favor. I want you to find your pulse. Go ahead… find it. Do you feel that? Beat… Beat… Beat… Beat… You feel it?

Let me ask you: You feel that this life is your own? You still think that you are in control of your life? You feel that pulse of yours? What in the world do you have to do with that? It began beating the moment God said, and it will stop beating the moment God says.

You should know that while your pulse is still beating, you have the opportunity to come and be absolutely Soul'd Out to God. However, the moment your pulse stops beating, it is too late.

Verses to Meditate On:

"I myself no longer live, but Christ lives in me. So I live my life in this earthly body by trusting in the Son of God, who loved me and gave Himself for me."
- Galatians 2:20

"But my life is worth nothing unless I use it for doing the work assigned me by the Lord Jesus – the work of telling others the Good News about God's wonderful kindness and love."
- Acts 20:24

"I once thought all these things were so very important, but now I consider them worthless because of what Christ has done. Yes, everything else is worthless when compared with the priceless gain of knowing Christ Jesus my Lord. I have discarded everything else, counting it all as garbage, so that I may have Christ."
- Philippians 3:7-8

"This is why the Lord says, 'Turn to me now, while there is time! Give Me your hearts. Come with fasting, weeping, and mourning. Don't tear your clothing in your grief; instead, tear your hearts.' Return to the Lord your God, for He is gracious and merciful. He is not easily angered. He is filled with kindness and is eager not to punish you."
- Joel 2:12-13

"I heard about You before, but now I have seen You with my own eyes. I take back everything I said, and I sit in dust and ashes to show my repentance."

- Job 42:5 - 6

Father, thank You for opening my eyes and mind to the reality that this life is not about me. Lord, help me to continue realizing that no excuse is worth getting in the way of Your calling in this life.

Also, thank You for helping me to understand that the length of my days is completely in Your hands. Teach me to die to myself more and more each of those days, because I know that if I want to be completely Soul'd Out to You, I must die to myself. - Amen

CHAPTER 4

NOT FOR SALE

"you must shoulder your cross…"
– Matthew 16:24

Today, the cross is the most popular symbol in the entire civilized world, and in America the cross, as a piece of jewelry, far exceeds sports, arts, or other systems of belief in sales. There are literally millions of people who wear this symbol on their t-shirts, around their necks, and on their bodies with permanent ink.

I will be the first to admit that it's wonderful to see the cross so widely recognized and accepted. However, I must ask the questions, "Do people really understand what the cross is all about? Do they truly get the concept of what it means to wear a cross?"

In his book, *Power of the Cross,* Tim LaHaye shared some of the same concerns, so when he would came across someone wearing a cross as a piece of jewelry, he would approach them, and ask them two questions:

1.   Why do you wear that cross?
2.   What does it mean to you?[11]

I would like to share some of the responses that Dr. LaHaye received:

One woman waiting to enter a restaurant said of her cross, "I saw it in the display case of a shop and thought it was attractive. Because it was on sale for 50 percent off, I bought it." And what did it mean to her? "It means I am a religious person who respects all religions."[12]

A young clerk wearing a beautiful gold cross on a gold chain around her neck said, "My boyfriend gave it to me for Christmas, and I love him very much. I wear it because it reminds me of him."[13]

Another man was dressed in a gray athletic sweatshirt and pants and wore the biggest silver cross I have ever seen hanging around a person's neck. When I asked why he wore it, he replied, "My grandmother gave it to me for Christmas, and I am going to visit her this weekend. I knew she would expect me to wear it."

---

[11] Tim LaHaye, *Power of the Cross* (Sisters, OR: Multnomah Books, 1998), 29.

[12] *Ibid.*, 30.

[13] *Ibid.*

And what did it mean to him? "Absolutely nothing!" End of conversation.[14]

You would have to wonder, does anyone understand what the cross is all about? Is there anyone out there who really cares? After reading these three previous testimonies, the outlook seems pretty hopeless, doesn't it? However, there was this one answer that I read in Dr. LaHaye's book:

One woman tenderly held her cross and with tear-filled eyes said, "This cross means everything to me. Jesus Christ has saved me and changed my life." She mentioned her terrible past and said, "Had I not become a Christian, I probably wouldn't be alive today."[15]

This woman got it! She understood what the cross was all about, and how it demanded a change in her life.

The Beautiful Demanding Cross

The cross was the greatest act of love ever shown to mankind. "I command you to love each other in the same way that I love you. And here is how to measure it – the greatest love is shown when people lay down their lives for their friends." (John 15:12 – 13)

---

[14] *Ibid.*, 31.
[15] *Ibid.*, 33.

On the cross, the Son of God laid down His life for us because He loved His creation so much that He wanted to make a way possible for us to be His friends. Through the cross, God made the way possible to know Him intimately right now, and to spend the rest of our lives walking with Him.

You must understand that Christ did not step out of Heaven, live a perfect life, lay down His life on a cross in your place, and then rise again three days later just so you wouldn't have to go to Hell! It is so important for us all to realize that we don't turn from our sin and place our faith in the Son of God so that we can go to Heaven when we die. Of course, if we are born again, the moment we draw our last breath, we will be with God in Heaven for all of eternity. This is the reward at the end of our life when we are born again through Christ.

However, the cross represents an opportunity for us to walk with Christ in a relationship RIGHT NOW! Not waiting until you die, but RIGHT NOW! If the cross was just about escaping Hell and getting to go to Heaven, then the moment you gave your life to Christ it would only make sense for you to ascend to Heaven at that very minute. But, guess what? You are still here, and so are millions of other born again Christians.

What took place on the cross of Christ two thousand years ago will set you free from the bondage of sin the very moment you give Him the throne of your heart. Therefore, this cross deserves top priority today and every day after today.

The Cross for Every Day

In Matthew 16:24, Jesus told His disciples that they must "shoulder their cross." He was teaching them that part of being Soul'd Out to Him was carrying their cross every day. This statement would have struck a chord with the disciples two thousand years ago that would have been quite different from what we understand today.

I can only imagine the eye-opening thoughts that raced through the disciples' heads after those words proceeded from Jesus' mouth.

The cross was a shameful and torturous killing machine. Just to mention the cross would send fear racing up the spine because it was a device that no one wanted to come in contact with.

But here is the Son of God telling His disciples to shoulder their cross every day. It would be like me telling you today "to shoulder your electric chair everyday" or "to carry your cyanide daily."

He was telling His disciples that they must die daily. They are no longer living as themselves, but rather they are dying and must continue dying every day. To be absolutely Soul'd Out to Jesus Christ meant they must die to themselves and shoulder the very cross that had killed their flesh!

This same truth applies to us two thousand years later. If we're going to be completely Soul'd Out to the Son of God, then we must become walking dead men and women. We don't just die once to the cross, and then live the rest of our lives the way we want to till we die. But rather we have to shoulder our cross and die daily. You see, Jesus is not asking people to just add Him to the agendas of their lives. He wants disciples that are willing to be dead to their flesh every day.

Ryan Dobson issues this challenge: "Where He is, we're to be. Jesus is saying, because I go to the cross, I want you to go to the cross. If I die, you die. If you're really My follower, My servant, then you have no other option."[16]

You want to be completely Soul'd Out to Christ? Then shoulder your cross daily!

---

[16] Ryan Dobson, *2 Die 4* (Sisters, OR: Multnomah Publishers, 2004), 15.

A Man Easily Bought

There are several Bible names that you'll probably never hear anyone name their child again. There are some people in the Bible who brought eternal shame to their names, and scared future generations forever. For example: Jezebel, Cain, Nebuchadnezzar, and the most infamous of them all, Judas. Could you picture walking up to a new mom with a beautiful baby boy and asking her, "What is your son's name?" And she replies, "His name is Judas!" No, probably something you'll never hear!

Judas Iscariot brought eternal shame to his name, because he Soul'd Out to something far less valuable than Jesus Christ. Judas did not die to himself and carry his cross, so he had a cost and was bought for a price of destruction.

Have you ever played the absurd game where you ask someone if they would do a ridiculous stunt for a certain amount of money? For example, "For a hundred dollars, would you walk through your local mall with a big yellow chicken costume on yelling 'eggs are yummy?'" I have to sadly admit that I've spent literally hours going back and forth with my brother-in-law over different dares such as this. I'm sure you don't want to admit it also, but you've most likely played this game as well.

Basically what we are asking in this game is "how much is it going to take for you to become a fool?" What is your cost? Everyone has his or her cost, right? Everyone has his or her price tag. Judas Iscariot had a cost. What is your cost?

Judas Sells Out

In Matthew 26:14-16, it records the story of Judas selling out.

"Then Judas Iscariot, one of the twelve disciples, went to the leading priests and asked, 'How much will you pay me to betray Jesus to you?' And they gave him thirty pieces of silver. From that time on, Judas began looking for the right time and place to betray Jesus."
                                    - Matthew 26:14-16

The Jewish leaders had been seeking a way to get Jesus for some time now, so you can imagine their excitement when supposedly "one of His own" came to them. These leading priests found out quickly what Judas's cost would be. They bought him off for thirty pieces of silver - the exact buying cost for the average slave of that time period. Isn't it ironic that Judas was a slave to his self-interest, so he sells the Son of God for the exact same price of a slave?

Judas Seeks Opportunity to Cash In

The account in Matthew continues to say, "From that time on, Judas began looking for the right time and place to betray Jesus." (Matthew 26:16) His perfect opportunity came when Jesus went to pray in the Garden of Gethsemane.

The question has to be: "Why? Why would he do that? Why would Judas sell out for merely thirty pieces of silver?" This was not a lot of money at that time. In fact, Jesus had made him treasurer over the disciple's moneybox, so he could've gladly helped himself to it anytime he wanted to. In the Gospel of John, it suggests that he did this very act several times. "Not that he cared for the poor – he was a thief who was in charge of the disciples' funds, and he often took some for his own use." (John 12:6)

So, did Judas do it because he was money hungry? Possibly! Maybe he did it because he thought his betrayal would force Jesus to overthrow the Roman Empire that had oppressed the Jews for some time. It is possible that Judas thought Jesus was a false Messiah, because He was more interested in setting people free spiritually than He was in setting them free physically. Maybe it is because Jesus had talked about dying, and Judas believed the true Messiah could not die!

What is the real reason Judas sold Jesus out? We really don't know. However, there is one thing that we do know. Judas had a cost, and this cost ended up costing him his soul!

Another truth that we can learn from Judas's eternal mistake is that he was able to be bought, because he was not Soul'd Out to Christ. He had not died to himself, and he wasn't shouldering his cross daily. So when the time came, Judas was bought with a small price, and a lot of ease!

Judas was not Soul'd Out to Christ, so he had a cost. What is your cost?

What is Your Cost?

Every single one of us has to face the ugly reality that we may be a potential Judas. Are you someone that is seeking the right opportunity to betray Christ and walk away? You don't have to intentionally plan on selling out to be bought. Many people will walk away from God without necessarily realizing it. I have seen numerous teenagers who were really into church and serving Christ; then a new boyfriend or girlfriend came into the picture and they stopped being seen around. I have seen others who grew up in church and went through the youth group. Then once they went off to college and got away from their parents and their home church, they stopped going altogether.

I have seen many adults who traded serving Christ for a new well-paying job. There are others who allow a new group of friends or organized sports to buy them out. (I'm often amazed by those who will not miss a church softball game for the world, but will allow any little 'ole thing to keep them away from a worship service.) Why do so many of us trade the joy of being completely Soul'd Out to God for things far less valuable?

So what is your cost? What opportunity are you waiting on to come across your offering table before you walk away? Is going off to college your price? What about a member of the opposite sex? Popularity and prosperity? Are you just waiting for another Christian or minister to upset you before you walk away?

What is your price? What can you be bought for?

Those Who are Soul'd Out Don't Have a Cost

If you are truly and completely Soul'd Out, then you should realize that you don't have a cost. You cannot be bought because you are not for sale! If you understand that you are God's redeemed child, you must know that you belong to Him and you cannot sell what doesn't belong to you!

Let's say you go to a garage sale or a flea market, and you see an item that sparks your interest. As you walk up to this particular item, you notice there is a big sign on it that simply says, "Sold." What would you do? Well, I will tell you what you would do. You would do what we all would do. You would walk away because the item is no longer for sale because someone else has bought it.

That's exactly what it means to "shoulder your cross daily." When you are carrying your cross daily, it means that you are dying daily. Your life is no longer yours to sell because it has been bought with a price by Christ. "You do not belong to yourself, for God bought you with a high price. So you must honor God with your body." (1 Corinthians 6:19b – 20)

When temptation comes up to you, it should see a huge sign on you that says, "Not for sale. I'm already sold." When Satan approaches you, he should see your cross and realize you're not for sale. When evil comes knocking at your door, it shouldn't receive an answer because you've already been bought by the King of Kings.

I am reminded of a story that C. A. Roberts wrote in his book, *This Way to the Cross*, of a young priest who had come to a point in his life where he was ready to sell out.

Several years ago there was a disturbed young priest at the University of Paris. He came one day to make his confession. He sat down in the booth and began to talk, casually and aimlessly. There was an older and much wiser priest beyond the screen. The older minister realized the boy did not have his mind on what he was saying.

Presently, he interrupted the boy to say, "Young man, you don't mean a thing you are saying, do you?" The boy, at first startled, shot back an answer. "You are right. I don't. And I'll tell you why. I'm fed up with this whole business of religion. It doesn't make a bit of sense to me. I'm fed up with these rules and restrictions; I'm fed up with all this ritualism; I'm fed up with this booth; and I'm fed up with people like you. I want to get out."

The older priest replied, "Then, son, I think you should. But if you are getting out, make a break clean. Don't simply go half way." He paused a moment and continued. "To show you what I mean, I want you to do one last thing before you go. Will you do it?"

The boy replied, "If I can."

The priest explained his request. "I want you to go across the street to the Cathedral of Notre Dame. I want you to go inside and make your way down to the altar. There you will find the life-size replica of Christ hanging on the cross. I want you to stand there and look up into His face. Then say aloud, 'I did this to you and I do not care.'"

The boy said he would do it. He left the building, crossed the street, and entered the Cathedral. He made his way down the aisle. He had never been inside the church when it was completely empty. There was no chanting. There was no music. The silence was almost suffocating.

Finally, he found himself standing before the altar. He looked up at the replica of the cross. After an eternal moment, he began, "I did this to You" – but he did not finish. A second time he began, "I did this to You" – and a second time he did not finish. The third time he did not look up. Slowly, he dropped to his knees, bowed his head, and said, "O God, I did this to You, and *I do care*!"[17]

This young priest recognized that Jesus gave all for him, so he could do nothing short of giving his all for Him. It no longer mattered to this young man how tired or frustrated he got because he now realized that it was no longer about him. He had died, and he was going to be Soul'd Out to Christ for the rest of his life, no matter what!

---

[17] C. A. Roberts, *This Way to the Cross* (Nashville, TN: Broadman Press, 1966), 21 – 23.

Are you willing to "shoulder your cross" daily? Are you willing to be Soul'd Out to Him? If you are willing, then it means you're going to say "no" to whatever your flesh is telling you to do in opposition to what God says. It means constantly letting go of what your flesh wants to hold on to when God says surrender it.[18]

The *me* in you needs to be put on the cross. Put to death. Crucified. So go, and die daily!

Verses to Meditate On:

"For to me, living is for Christ, and dying is even better."
- Philippians 1:21

"We are well known, but we are treated as unknown. We live close to death, but we are, still live. We have been beaten within an inch of our lives."
- 2 Corinthians 6:9

"Our sinful selves were crucified with Christ so that sin might lose its power in our lives. We are no longer slaves to sin. For when we died with Christ we were set free from the power of sin."
- Romans 6:6-7

---

[18] Ryan Dobson, *2 Die 4*, 64.

"And I heard a voice from heaven saying, 'Write this down: Blessed are those who die in the Lord from now on. Yes says the Spirit, they are blessed indeed, for they will rest from their toils and trials; for their good deeds follow them!'"

- Revelation 14:13

"Jesus told her, 'I am the resurrection and the life. Those who believe in Me, even though they die like everyone else, will live again."

- John 11:25

Father, thank You for helping me to realize that I must die daily if You are going to use me in amazing ways. I want to live a life that is glorifying to You, and I now understand that I can't do that as long as my flesh is alive in me.

Lord, help me to shoulder my cross and continue to die daily to this world, my wants, and my desires. You have bought me and I am no longer for sale! Thank You, Father, for purchasing me. - Amen

CHAPTER 5

I'M A FOLLOWER

"and follow Me!" – Matthew 16:24

We began in Chapter 1 discussing the fact that our lives are meant to know God, and to exalt Him forever. That this in fact is the purpose for your existence, and the very reason why you're here on earth: To be Soul'd Out to the King of the Universe. "Everything has been created through Him and for Him." (Colossians 1:16b)

Then, we discussed in Chapter 2 that there is Someone worth following, and His name is Jesus Christ. We are to be Soul'd Out to Him because He is the most valuable treasure there is.

In Chapter 3, we followed with the truth that if we are going to be Soul'd Out to Christ, then we must die. You cannot fully embrace Him for all that He is until your ambitions and desires are out of the picture.

Secondly, in Chapter 4, we talked about shouldering your cross daily. You must continue to die every day that you're here. When you're dying every day, you can't be bought by temptation, sin, or Satan, because you are already Soul'd to Christ.

Finally, in Chapter 5, we can discuss the excitement of following Jesus wherever He leads us. You are now able, for the first time, to do what you were created to do. You can now fulfill your purpose for existence. You can be truly Soul'd Out!

Christ has "called" every single one of us to be Soul'd Out to Him and to follow Him. He "called" you with a special summons to walk with Him, even before He created the world. "For we are God's masterpiece. He has created us anew in Christ Jesus, so that we can do the good things He planned for us long ago." (Ephesians 2:10)

Os Guinness exposed it magnificently in his book, *Rising to the Call,* when he said, "Calling is the truth that God calls us to Himself so decisively that everything we are, everything we do, and everything we have is invested with a special devotion, dynamism, and direction lived out as a response to His summons and service."[19] He has called you, and now you're ready to follow. How exciting!

---

[19] Os Guinness, *Rising to the Call* (Nashville, TN: W Publishing Group, 2003), 21.

Following In Power

Have you ever seen a movie that actually showed one of the closing scenes at the very beginning, and then the rest of the movie describes how the story or character got to that point?

I am going to take you on a brief ride through the disciple Peter's life and transformation. He became a man who was a very powerful and dangerous tool for God's kingdom. He was absolutely Soul'd Out to Christ, and God did the miraculous through him.

In the book of Acts, it records of Peter:

"And more and more people believed and were brought to the Lord – crowds of both men and women. As a result of the apostle's work, sick people were brought out into the streets on beds and mats so that Peter's shadow might fall across some of them as he went by. Crowds came in from the villages around Jerusalem, bringing their sick and those possessed by evil spirits, and they were all healed."
                                                              - Acts 5:14-16

Wow! Here is a man, just an ordinary man, who was overflowing with the power of God. And the people of Jerusalem recognized Peter as someone who was obviously plugged into the Almighty.

They were literally laying sick people out in the streets hoping that the shadow of this disciple would shade their afflictions. The multitudes were flocking to him, not because there was any power that Peter had on his own, but instead they wanted to be touched by his God. Simon Peter was completely Soul'd Out, and everyone knew that Christ's power was oozing from his pores!

However, this was not always the case with him. Let's take a quick look into the biography of this man's life to see what brought him to the point of being absolutely Soul'd Out for the Son of God.

A Zero Who Needed A Hero

Before we really jump into this section about Peter, I would like to start off with a simple truth about him. You will see this truth laid out while we scan through several narratives in the gospels.

Truth: *When Peter was in the direct presence of Jesus, he had amazing power! Near his Christ, Peter would say and do the miraculous! When he was around his Hero, the Son of God, Peter became a hero. However, when he was away from Jesus, or took his eyes off Him, he would fall on his face and totally make a mess of things. Away from the direct presence of Jesus, Peter was an absolute zero.*

Example #1

"Immediately after this, Jesus made his disciples get back into the boat and cross to the other side of the lake while He sent the people home. Afterward He went up into the hills by Himself to pray. Night fell while He was there alone. Meanwhile, the disciples were in trouble far away from the land, for a strong wind had risen, and they were fighting heavy waves.

About three o'clock in the morning Jesus came to them, walking on the water. When the disciples saw Him, they screamed in terror, thinking He was a ghost. But Jesus spoke to them at once. 'It is all right,' He said. 'I am here! Don't be afraid.'

Then Peter called to Him, 'Lord, if it's really You, tell me to come to You by walking on water.'

'All right, come,' Jesus said.

So Peter went over the side of the boat and walked on the water toward Jesus. But when He looked around at the high waves, he was terrified and began to sink. 'Save me, Lord!' He shouted.

Instantly Jesus reached out His hand and grabbed Him, 'You don't have much faith,' Jesus said. 'Why did you doubt Me?' And when they climbed back into the boat, the wind stopped."

- Matthew 14:22-33

This is an amazing account here. This event takes place on the Sea of Galilee. (I recently had the opportunity to go to Israel and take a boat ride across the Sea, so I can just imagine the scene as I am writing.) Here are Peter and the boys floating across the sea, and a violent storm brews up. Around three o'clock in the morning, they see a figure walking across the raging sea, who turns out to be Jesus.

By the time this story occurs, I believe Peter had begun to realize that he was a different person when he was close to Christ. On several occasions, he had probably reasoned within himself, "When I am around Jesus, I seem to do really well, but when I am away from Him, I am constantly eating my sandals!" Peter had definitely grown to love being where his Messiah was.

I truly believe this is the reason why he asked if he could get out of the boat and walk on the raging sea towards his Savior. I mean honestly, why wouldn't he just wait until Jesus got to the boat? After all, He was walking in that direction! However, Peter jumped out of the boat with this thought that I think was rushing through his head, "I am here, He is there. That is not a good thing. I want to be where He is! I must be close to Him!"

So here goes Peter right over the edge of the boat into the water, and he walks on the Sea of Galilee. Did you hear what I said? Peter was walking on the Sea of Galilee! I don't know about you, but that is not something I see every day! I have to admit that I thought I saw someone running on water one day, but as my heart was pounding out of my chest I realized they were just skiing!

Simon Peter was watching his Christ and he was doing the miraculous. He had his eyes on the King of Kings as he got closer and closer to Him. Because of this, he was defying the natural law of gravity. When he jumped out of the boat, it never crossed his mind that he could not walk on water. He just wanted to get to Jesus, and that is all that mattered. What a miracle!

However, after a couple of minutes I believe it began to hit Peter as to what he was really doing. He began to take his eyes off Jesus, and began looking at the waves around him. He started focusing on the spray of water that was now hitting him in the face, instead of remembering that the very Creator of that Sea was the One who had called him out there.

Instead of thinking about getting near Christ, he thought, "Hey, I don't walk on water! What am I doing out here?" Because Peter had taken his eyes off Jesus, he began to sink.

In wrapping up this example, I want you to see what happens next. Peter cries out for help and Jesus pulls him up out of the water. Then they both walk back to the boat and climb inside. I have often pictured this scene as Jesus lifting Peter up and slinging him on His back piggyback style, then carrying him back to the boat, but this is not what the bible says happened. They both walked back. When Peter got into the arms of Jesus, he was once again focused on his Hero, and began walking on water yet another time back to the boat!

When Peter is in the direct presence of his Messiah he does the miraculous. However, when he takes his eyes off his Hero, he is a zero with the rim knocked off. He is absolutely nothing!

Example #2

"When Jesus came to the region of Caesarea Philippi, he asked His disciples, 'Who do people say that the Son of Man is?'

'Well', they replied, 'some say John the Baptist, some say Elijah, and others say Jeremiah or one of the other prophets.'

Then He asked them, 'Who do you say I am?'

Simon Peter answered, 'You are the Messiah, the Son of the living God.'

Jesus replied, 'You are blessed, Simon son of John, because my Father in Heaven has revealed this to you. You did not learn this from any human being.'

- Matthew 16:13-17

In this situation Jesus and His disciples were walking through a certain city that evidently thought a whole lot about two men: Caesar and King Philip. Hence the name of the city, Caesarea Philippi. In fact, there were said to have been two huge statues of the men right in the middle of the city. Jesus and His disciples very well may have been looking at these two statues when He asked them the question, "What do people think about Me?"

The disciples reported the popular consensus going around about Him. Then Jesus asked them, "Okay, who do you say that I am?" And Peter let it rip! He did not wait and think about his answer before he let it fly because he would've probably messed up once again if he had thought about it too much. He just blurted out, "You are the Messiah, the Son of the living God!"

I can imagine Peter thinking, "Where in the world did that come from? That answer just came to me, and within a split second it was coming out of my mouth!" Well, Jesus tells Simon Peter where the answer came from: "You are blessed, Simon son of John, because My Father in Heaven has revealed this to you. You did not learn this from any human being (v. 17)." The Son of God was telling Peter, "That was not you who spoke, but My Father in Heaven just spoke through you!"

Here is Simon Peter in the presence of his Savior, and he's speaking the miraculous words of God. At the side of his Savior, Peter is used in awesome ways. Away from his Hero, Peter is an absolute zero!

Still not getting the point about following Christ? Let me give you some more examples from Peter's life.

Example #3

In Mark 14:32-42, Jesus and the disciples are in the Garden of Gethsemane. Jesus leaves them and goes a bit further into the Garden to pray. He told them to stay there and pray, as well.

However, here is Peter away from the direct presence of Jesus. So what do you think Peter was doing? Praying, right? Nope! He was away from his Savior, and he was sleeping!

When Peter is away from Jesus, he's an absolute failure. He can't even stay awake. He's worthless!

Example #4

In Matthew 26:47-56, Peter is back in the presence of his Hero and he becomes a fearless warrior! Judas is coming with a band of soldiers numbering well over five hundred. As they are approaching, Peter pulls out a small knife, and with Jesus by his side, he is going to take on all of them!

Although Jesus rebukes him for trying to take matters into his own hands by striking a man in the ear, Peter was still courageous with his Hero there by his side.

With the Son of God around him, Peter is a man who is scared of absolutely no one. He is courageous, fearless, and ready to take on the world.

Example #5

However, in Matthew 26:69-75, Peter is away from his Hero once again, because He had been arrested. The man who was going to take on over five hundred men is now fearful of a servant girl. This Simon Peter, who was fearless with Jesus by his side, is now denying he even knows Him. The young servant girl had put him on the spot.

Peter is falling on his face once again! Why? Because he is away from his Messiah. Apart from Jesus, Peter is a coward, a liar, and a failure. He has to have his Hero there!

What's A Man To Do?

I think by now we have successfully established the truth of Peter's uselessness and failures apart from Christ. You take Peter away from Jesus, and he is nothing! Worthless! He is a zero with the rim knocked off! And by this point, Peter surely realized how badly he needed the Son of God. But what is a man to do?

We know that later a group of people condemned and sentenced Jesus to be put to death. He was then crucified and buried. However, He rose again the third day, appeared for forty days to various people, and then He ascended into Heaven. But, this is terrible news for Peter right? Surely, he thought to himself, "When I'm away from the presence of my Hero I constantly mess up. Jesus is gone! What am I going to do? I'm done!"

However, just days later this same Peter stands and begins to preach to thousands of the very same people who have crucified his Hero. "Then Peter stepped forward with the eleven other apostles and shouted to the crowd, 'Listen carefully, all of you, fellow Jews and residents of Jerusalem! Make no mistake about this...'" (Acts 2:14)

He continued to deliver one of the best sermons ever preached right in the middle of the city, and the Bible recorded that there were about three thousand people who became Soul'd Out to Christ that very day. (Acts 2:41-42)

So what happened? What had changed? Wasn't Jesus in Heaven now, and away from Peter?

Well, Jesus had promised something to the disciples before He was crucified:

"And I will ask the Father, and He will give you another Counselor, who will never leave you. He is the Holy Spirit, who leads into all truth. The world at large cannot receive Him, because it isn't looking for Him and doesn't recognize Him. But you do, because He lives with you now and later will be in you. No, I will not abandon you as orphans - I will come to you."

- John 14:16-18

When Jesus ascended to Heaven, the Holy Spirit came. Peter was filled with the Holy Spirit in Acts 2, so that meant that he had all the same power and more because he no longer was standing side by side with Jesus. Now, His Spirit was living inside of him!

For the rest of his life, everything Peter did, he did as though he were in the direct presence of his Hero. God was no longer working beside him, but through Him!

"And more and more people believed and were brought to the Lord - crowds of both men and women. As a result of the apostles' work, sick people were brought out into the streets on beds and mats so that Peter's shadow might fall across some of them as he went by. Crowds came in from the villages around Jerusalem, bringing their sick and those possessed by evil spirits, and they were all healed."
- Acts 5:14-16

For Peter, being absolutely Soul'd Out was living every moment as though he were walking in the direct presence of God. His ability to follow Christ in this way caused all of Jerusalem to recognize him as a man that was overflowing with the power of God. This truth caused them to come out to the streets and find out more about Peter's Hero!

Follow Him Like He's There...

You know what? I wanted to use this illustration of Peter's life because we are all just like him. You take Jesus away from us, and we're absolutely nothing as well. When you are not following the Son of God, you are also a zero with the rim knocked off. If I'm not Soul'd Out to Him, then I'm worthless!

Whether you like to admit it or not, you know exactly what I'm talking about. You have tried doing everything on your own, and you're failing completely. It seems like the harder you try, the harder you fall on your face. The more you try to say, the more you taste your own shoe!

Well, that is what this whole book has been dealing with. Give up! Die! Surrender! Sell out! Stop, quit, and commit your life right now to become less and less like yourself every day, and to become more and more like Christ everyday! "He must become greater and greater, and I must become less and less." (John 3:30)

That is how you truly follow Him. Live your life becoming just like Jesus Christ because you are now living in His direct presence every day. If you have turned from your sin and have placed your trust in Him as your Master, then you must recognize that He is living inside of you at this very moment.

Where He is, you are. Where He goes, you go. Where He leads, you follow. What He does, you do. Thomas a' Kempis issued an amazing charge in his work, *Imitation of Christ*:

"I had rather be poor for Your sake than rich without You. I prefer rather to wander on the earth with You than to possess Heaven without You. Where You are there is Heaven, and where You are not are death and Hell. You are my desire and therefore I must cry after You and sigh and pray. In none can I fully trust to help me in my necessities, but in You alone, my God. You are my hope. You are my confidence. You are my Consoler, most faithful in every need."[20]

He is there. He is with you. Following Him is being with Him at all times, and being Soul'd Out to Him is realizing that being with Him is the best thing in the entire world!

Go And Be Soul'd Out

Someone is reported to have asked a concert violinist in New York's Carnegie Hall how she became so skilled. She said that it was by "planned neglect." She planned to neglect everything that was not related to her goal.[21] If you are going to push past mediocrity, and follow Him in complete devotion, then neglect anything that gets in your way. Your goal is to be absolutely Soul'd Out to Him, so anything that is between you and that goal, you must say "Buh-By" to it! He's worth it!

---

[20] Thomas a' Kempis, *Imitation of Christ* (Nashville, TN: Thomas Nelson Publishers, 1999), 132.
[21] John MacArthur Jr., *Found: God's Will* (Colorado Springs, CO: Victor Books, 1973), 30.

In The Practice of the Presence of God, Brother Lawrence penned:
"This made me resolve to give all for the All, so after having given myself wholly to God, to make all the satisfaction I could for my sins, I renounced, for the love of Him, everything that was not He; and I began to live as if there was none but He and I in the world."[22]

Do you want to be used in unexplainable ways by God? Want to live a life that is fulfilling its purpose? Want to be a follower of Christ while being completely Soul'd Out to Him? Then give your all for the All. Renounce anything that gets in your way of that goal, and realize He is right there inside you.

Is the world yet to see what God will do with someone, or a generation that is fully Soul'd Out to Him? Then, you go and be that someone! Push past mediocrity! Go and turn this world upside down for Jesus Christ, the King of Kings, the Lord of Lords, the Son of God, the Savior of the world!

---

[22] Brother Lawrence, *The Practice of the Presence of God* (Peabody, MA: Hendrickson Publishers Inc., 2004), 26.

Verses to Meditate On:

"I follow close behind you; Your strong right hand holds me securely."
- Psalm 63:8

"As Jesus was going down the road, He saw Matthew sitting at his tax-collection booth. 'Come, be My disciple,' Jesus said to him. So Matthew got up and followed Him.
- Matthew 9:9

"My sheep recognize My voice; I know them, and they follow Me. I give them eternal life, and they will never perish. No one will snatch them away from Me."
- John 10:27

"Follow God's example in everything you do, because you are His dear children."
- Ephesians 5:1

"This suffering is all part of what God has called you to. Christ, who suffered for you, is your example. Follow in His steps."
- 1 Peter 2:21

"Then Jesus said to the disciples, 'If any of you wants to be My follower, you must put aside your selfish ambition, shoulder your cross, and follow Me. If you try to keep your life for yourself, you will lose it. But if you give up your life for Me, you will find true life.'"

- Matthew 16:24 - 25

Father, I now realize the reason for my existence is to know You and to glorify You. Thank you for opening my eyes to the reality that You are the most valuable Treasure in the entire world. You are worth following! Help me, Father, to die daily to myself, so that I can follow You full-heartedly.

Lord, set a deep burning passion within me that desires to become more like You every day. Each new day, I want to be more like You than I was the day before.

Lastly, Lord, I pray that you will use me in a miraculous way. I want to be that person who is fully consecrated to you. Make me to be absolutely SOUL'D OUT TO YOU, JESUS!!! - Amen

LAST WORD

I hope and pray that this book has been a huge challenge to you. Please allow me to encourage you in your continuing Soul'd Out walk with God. He is infinitely good, and I hope that you will enjoy His goodness as He met with you in this work.

If you have completed reading this book, then I would like you to e-mail me and share your thoughts, victories, concerns, etc. E-mail me at: **burn4himministries@yahoo.com**

I also want you to know that I've been praying for you. I prayed that each and every day you would become truly alive in Christ as you continually die to yourself.

In Christ,
Shane Pruitt
Matthew 16:24